Love is a Radiant Light
The Life & Words of St. Charbel

Love is a
Radiant Light

The Life & Words
of
St. Charbel

Hanna Skandar

Translated by
William J. Melcher

✻ Angelico Press

For information, address:
Angelico Press
169 Monitor St.
Brooklyn, NY 11222
www.angelicopress.com

ISBN: 978-1-62138-432-8 pbk
ISBN: 978-1-62138-433-5 cloth
ISBN: 978-1-62138-434-2 ebook

Cover Design: Michael Schrauzer

CONTENTS

HOMILIES (cont'd)

LIFE OF
SAINT CHARBEL

Journey of a Life

Childhood

Youssef antoun makhlouf, who later took the religious name of Charbel,[†] was born on May 8, 1828, in Bekaa Kafra.[‡] His parents provided their five children with a very pious Christian education.

At that time Lebanon was under Turkish occupation, and his father died after finishing a compulsory job for the Turkish army on August 8, 1831. After his mother remarried in October 1833, Youssef remained in Bekaa Kafra in his parents' house, under the guardianship of his paternal uncle Anthony. He learned to read and write from the priests of the village.

From his earliest youth, he always had a prayer book with him. He prayed, went to confession, and received Holy Communion frequently. Because of his piety, his

---

[†] A Syriac name derived from the contraction of two words: *Sharb*, which means story or account, and *El*, which means God; the name Charbel means: the story or account of God.

[‡] This is the highest village in Lebanon, situated at an altitude of 1,700 meters [5,575 feet] in the mountains to the north of the country, dominating the famous Valley of Kadisha, "the valley of the saints."

fondness for prayer, the Mass, and processions, his desire to avoid associating with people, and his good behavior, the people of the village used to call him "the saint."

Monastic Life

His maternal uncle, Father Daniel, traveled one day to Bekaa Kafra to visit his family. When he returned to the monastery of Our Lady in Mayfouq, he brought with him Youssef, who entered the novitiate on August 8, 1851, radiant with joy.

At the end of a one-year novitiate, Youssef joined Saint Maron Monastery in Annaya, where he entered the Lebanese Maronite Order (O.L.M.), taking the name Charbel, after a second-century martyr of the Church of Antioch. On November 1, 1853, he pronounced his solemn vows of poverty, chastity, and obedience.

His superiors then sent him to the Theological Institute of Saints Cyprian and Justina in Kfifan, to study for the priesthood. Brother Charbel was then considered very intelligent, one of the best students, excelling particularly in theology.

Brother Charbel was ordained a priest on July 23, 1859. He left then for the monastery of Saint Yaaqoub Al Hosson, where he lived as a hermit and was formed by asceticism and prayer.

The hermit Alichaa called for him to join him in Annaya. Father Charbel lived for sixteen years at Saint Maron Monastery in Annaya. Then he answered the call to solitary life and spent twenty-three years in a hermitage in the service of his Lord.

On December 18, 1898, while he was celebrating Mass, he suffered a stroke and began an agony that lasted six days, during which he remained at peace. In his agony, Father Charbel unceasingly repeated the prayer that he had not been able to finish at Mass: "Father of truth, behold Your Son. . . ." He also repeated the names of Jesus, Mary, and Joseph, and also of Peter and Paul, patron saints of the hermitage. Charbel's soul went to heaven on December 24, 1898, Christmas Eve.

He is buried in the cemetery of Saint Maron Monastery in Annaya, where the multiplication of extraordinary events and miracles after his death drew crowds and aroused devotion in people of all religious confessions and throughout the world. He was beatified by Pope Paul VI on December 5, 1965, and canonized by the same pope on October 9, 1977.

Path of Holiness, Testimonies

Portrait

A s a result of his ascetical practices and vigils, his face had become emaciated but still showed signs of his cheerfulness and serenity of heart. It also had a serious character. It reflected his devotion and love of God, particularly during prayer. It drew all hearts to him.

Work

He worked with the brothers and the domestic servants in the fields and in the vineyard. He was painstaking at work until the bell rang for prayer. Then he knelt down on the stones to recite the office. His hands were calloused from the work.

Poverty

He dressed like the poorest of the poor. He never wore a new habit but humbly sought to use the habits discarded by his confreres. His monastic habit was patched and threadbare. He jealously cared for the belongings of the monastery so as not to throw anything away, however insignificant it might be, not even the beanstalks. If he saw a grape seed under a vine stock, or a crumb on the path, he would pick them up and bring them to the kitchen. He was as poor as a beggar. Even a poor man would not have taken his food, his bed, and his clothing. He considered all the goods of this world to be dust.

His "mattress" was stuffed with oak leaves and tree bark, covered with a sort of mat woven of goat hair, all of it covered with an old piece of felt. A log rolled up in black cloth taken from a habit was his pillow. On this very rough bed, without mattress or blanket, he slept summer and winter.

He deliberately assumed a foolish, half-witted appearance to hide his intellectual prowess and spiritual gifts. Despite his outstanding intellect, he let nothing of his knowledge appear in his words or in his writings. His only wealth was his love for God. Apart from that, there was nothing remarkable about his existence in the world.

Food

At the hermitage, he used to eat only once a day. His food was frugal: some salad with olives, the skins of potatoes. When he came to the monastery for provisions, he would start by choosing for himself the moldy bread that they used to throw to the dogs and the leftovers from the meals of the previous days, so as to present to his companion the fresh bread and the good food. Moreover he walked a half hour to fill the water jar at the spring in Annaya for his companions. For himself, he would draw water from the well of the hermitage to drink.

Sobriety

He was content to live in the state in which he found himself, without ever seeking to leave it; his only desire was to do God's will. Wherever his superiors sent him, he found his rest and his joy, seeing in all these services a sign of God's kindness, whether he was sweeping, cooking, or digging.

Education

He was an erudite man. On the intellectual level he was cultivated and intelligent. He knew Syriac, from which he translated some texts into Arabic. He was precise and convincing in his answers, because he had received an excellent formation in theology.

Humility

A few of his confreres made fun of his naïveté, without noticing that he in fact embodied an example of Christian perfection by striving to camouflage his virtue and to hide his good deeds. He was modesty incarnate. Father Charbel was saddened by praise from others, since he was human to all appearances but in reality living in heaven. He willingly accepted the disdain of others and felt joy when he was insulted. Although he was a priest, a theologian, and an elder member of the Order, he devoted himself to the hardest manual labor.

Silence

He exemplified the rule of silence, because no one saw him except at church or else at work. At work he did not converse with anyone. If someone asked him a question, he answered kindly, calmly, and briefly. His words were marked by a profound humility.

Joy

He was always happy, joyful in the Lord, cheerful, content with his state of life. He grumbled about neither the cold nor the heat and never complained about anything. He practiced asceticism until the last day of his life, joyfully, assiduously, and exultantly.

Hope

His hope in God was unshakable. He considered this life and all that it involves as a means of gaining Christ. Whatever was happening in the Order, it never influenced in the least his spiritual life or the services that he rendered. At the hermitage and at the monastery, he lived as though he was not present: all his thoughts were directed to God.

Mercy

He welcomed people with charity and confidence. He sympathized with their situation and prayed for them. His piety impressed many of the faithful, who unceasingly asked him to visit their sick relatives so as to pray for their healing and the salvation of their souls. Many believers, even Muslims, flocked to him, bottles of water in hand. He used to bless their water, which acquired prodigious power. The sick, the handicapped, the afflicted, and the suffering came to him in droves from all around to request his prayers for God's mercy, because they believed that God answered his prayers. The visitor who went to see him at the hermitage always returned happy and consoled.

Confession

He went to confession once a week. He heard the confessions of the faithful, who praised his zeal to educate them and his effective influence in their lives. His advice penetrated souls. He was more perceptive in spiritual matters than doctors of theology. His example exerted a great influence on others, both monks and lay persons. He did his best to sow hope in their hearts. He knew how to comfort the dying and to fill their heart with hope so that they could accept their departure from this world and be assured of the resurrection.

Prayer

Charbel's prayer life began with the celebration of Holy Mass, the high point of his day, in which he contemplated the Lord Jesus Christ under the consecrated species. He spoke to him in a heart-to-heart conversation, with extreme recollection and respect. He participated in all of the Divine Office and prayed for a long time each day. After midnight he used to kneel straight as a ramrod, immobile, with his hands crossed over his chest, having placed under his knees a wicker tray that he had crafted with his own hands, and he remained in that same posture throughout the recitation of the Holy Rosary.

Extraordinary Incidents

Father Charbel worked in the fields like the least of the domestics. One night, at harvest time, he was watching the goats while a group of around thirty volunteer harvesters ate at the monastery. Some servers were busying themselves around the tables. The cellarer was hurrying to serve the harvesters. Just then Father Charbel came up and asked him, in front of the whole crowd, to fill his lantern with oil.

The cellarer grumbled and said to him, "Why did you not come during the day?"

He answered, "I was in the fields!"

The cellarer retorted: "As punishment, I will not give you any oil for tonight. Go away!"

He obeyed and returned to his cell.

Saba, who was only thirteen years old, was at that time a domestic at the monastery. He visited him and asked for his lantern under the pretext of filling it with oil. But in fact he filled it with water.

Father Charbel took the lantern, lit it, and it flared up normally.

Then, in Father Charbel's absence, the superior issued an order forbidding the monks to light their lanterns after the bell marking the time to sleep. That night the superior woke up to attend to certain needs. As he went out he saw a light and discovered that it was Father Charbel's cell that was lit up.

He said to him, "Did you not hear the bell? Why did you not extinguish your lantern? Did you not take a vow of poverty?"

Immediately he knelt down to ask forgiveness and said, "I returned from the fields and I had to finish my prayers. I have not heard of this rule against lanterns!"

Saba, who was close to the cell, said to the superior, "I wanted to fill Father Charbel's lantern with oil, but the cellarer refused. As I came back, I saw that the can contained some ashes and water, and I filled his lantern with it!"

The superior opened it, emptied it, and made sure that it was in fact water. Then, deeply moved and unwilling to remain silent about his discovery, he went to tell someone about this incident, and the story spread through the monastery.

The following day, the superior called for Father Charbel and said to him, "If you want to go to the hermitage to serve the hermits, I see nothing wrong with that."

Father Charbel replied, "There is a big difference between my desire and the superior's order: if you order me to do it, I will obey and go there."

The superior replied, "Go!"

Father Charbel knelt down and asked for his blessing. The superior recited a prayer and blessed him. He stood up, expressed his gratitude, hurried to gather his spiritual books and breviaries, which he put into the mattress cover along with his blanket, tied everything up with a string, put his burden on his back, went into the church to visit the Blessed Sacrament, and then set off for the hermitage.

Toward Heaven

His Final Mass

QAFA, the wife of Saba Al-Ouwaïni, testified:

On December 16, 1898, I went with a group of people to participate in the Eucharist at the hermitage. Father Charbel began to celebrate Mass. But as soon as he had finished pronouncing the words of the consecration, an attack struck him down. Father Makarios, his companion, rushed over, removed his Mass vestments and helped him to stand up again. He found his place and continued the Mass. But no sooner had he elevated the Blessed Sacrament than he stiffened again. His companion noticed that Father Charbel was prolonging the elevation in an unusual way. He went over to him and found him in great pain. He gently removed the Host from his hand, placed it on the paten, and assisted by Brother Boutros, made him sit down on a chair near the altar. A half hour later, the crisis passed and he finished the Mass despite his illness.

The following Sunday, when we came into the church, we found Father Charbel prostrate, praying. At our request, a man went to ask about the hour of the Mass, because the weather was very cold and it was not possible to wait a long time.

Shortly after that, the hermit entered, wearing priestly vestments, and began. Before the words of the consecration, the same symptoms started again. They took off his Mass vestments, and he remained in the church to rest a bit. We were preparing to go back home, but Father Makarios stopped us, saying, "Do not leave, because Father Charbel is resting after experiencing an irregular heartbeat, and he will soon resume his Mass."

Then the hermit stood up again and continued the Mass.

He experienced discomfort several times; after resting for the third time, he resumed the Mass and tried to consume the Blood of Christ, but another crisis prevented him. With all his might he held the chalice and brought it close to his lips and teeth. He remained like that, stiff. When Father Makarios took the chalice away from him, Father Charbel had consumed the Blood of Christ.

They removed his Mass vestments and brought him into the monastic enclosure; he was only semiconscious. Nevertheless, he kept repeating: "O Father of Truth! O Jesus! O Mary! O Joseph!"

His companion stretched him out on a goat's hair carpet in the kitchen to warm him, because of the icy cold and the snow that had already accumulated to a height of more than a meter [three feet] around the hermitage. When they covered him, he would throw the blanket far away from him. When he regained consciousness, he said, "I want to say Mass; prepare the altar for me." He also said in Syriac: "Praise the Lord of heaven! Praise Him in the highest heaven! Lord, have mercy on me!"

He never stopped repeating these phrases during the six remaining days of his life. He died on Christmas Eve in 1898.

Toward the Tomb

The snow blocked access to the roads. The anxious monks said to each other: "Tomorrow will we be able to transfer the body to the tomb of the monastery, in such cold weather and in such a heavy snowstorm? Will we be able to announce his death in the surrounding areas?"

God's angels had announced that night the birth of the Savior to the shepherds in Bethlehem. They announced in the villages nearby Annaya that Father

Charbel had been born to eternal life. At nine o'clock they looked for a stretcher with a goat-hair cloth. Father Charbel's body was laid down on that cloth. The hermit, Father Makarios, arrived in tears, together with the brothers and the monks, and they put the body on the stretcher. Everyone was ready for the descent of the hermit toward Saint Maron Monastery along a gravel path that the young men had cleared, even though the snow continued to fall. Everyone was afraid that the stretcher might fall, so difficult it was to follow the path. Father Makarios said, "Let us trust in God! Have no fear! Father Charbel will make the way easier for us!"

When they carried him out of the hermitage, the clouds dispersed and the sun appeared in front of them, while behind them the snow fell. The cortège made its way without fatigue or difficulty, as though it were traveling a path that was not slippery. They all said: "This is one of Father Charbel's miracles!"

At 3:00 in the afternoon, the funeral services took place at the monastery. They were simple but very moving. The assembly repeated the words of Sacred Scripture: "Precious in the sight of the Lord is the death of his saints" (Ps 116:15).

The body was wrapped in a habit and buried, according to the custom of the monks, with no thought that it might be incorrupt.

The Light of the Resurrection

Some farmers testified:

> From the first night after his burial, we started
> to see from our houses, at a distance of a ten
> minutes' walk from the south side of the mon-
> astery, a brilliant light different from the ones
> that usually shine, something resembling an
> electric light. It would appear and disappear,
> keeping the same rhythm, as long as you
> looked at it. At first some said that this light
> came from lightning. In that light you could
> see better than in plain daylight the cupola and
> the east wall of the church, adjacent to the
> cemetery. We went to the monastery to tell
> the monks about this phenomenon. They did
> not believe us. Then we informed the superior
> about it. He too manifested his incredulity,
> telling us: "When you see the light, let some-
> one come and tell me! Or else send me a sig-
> nal."

The farmers agreed to the signal, and several times the
monks saw the lights that emerged from the tomb.

The Just Man Will Not See Corruption

Since spiritual lights were shooting from his tomb, it
was decided to open it. Father Alwan testified: "On the

eve of February 9, 1899, I went down to the tomb accompanied by Brother Elias and Saba Al-Ouwaïni. We opened the tomb, Father Charbel was lying on his back, his hands crossed over his chest; the body was in good condition."

The body was removed and placed in the nave of the church. The next day they found some water tinged with blood beneath the body and smelled a strong odor of mold. They placed the body in the cloister of the monastery on a goat's hair carpet, and Saba Al-Ouwaïni wiped away the mold with a cloth that he kept in his room. At first it smelled of mold, but then it started to emit a pleasant odor.

Father Joseph Al Kfouri set the body out on the terrace on the monastery roof for four months, exposed to the wind, so that the blood that oozed abundantly from his back and his hips could dry. He placed beneath it two white cloths that he changed every day. The blood continued to ooze copiously from his chest four months later, that is, from late spring until the end of summer.

They decided to display this surprising corpse in a cell of the monastery. Pilgrims came by the thousands, then by the tens of thousands, for twenty-three years, until 1921.

They venerated the loving, prayerful expression of that extraordinary body and collected the oily substance that it exuded, which healed and sometimes converted thousands of persons.

Nevertheless, in 1927 the Holy See ordered them to place the body in a tomb, in a cellar within the monastery. As an epitaph they simply wrote: "Here lies Father Charbel."

The Year 1950

Now in February 1950, fifty-two years after the death of Father Charbel, they noticed that without any possible explanation the same oozing was occurring through the thickness of the tomb.

The Father General then ordered that the tomb be opened. They began by opening a door that led to the church, so that the women could enter, since they had been forbidden to have access until then.

Emmanuel, the person who had opened the tomb, testifies:

> I began to dismantle the stones. . . . Then I went in, lantern in hand, and I saw the water draining from the coffin, which had become a small pool. . . . I asked for somebody to bring me the basin used for baptism along with some cloths. . . . I returned to lift the lid myself . . . . In front of me was a man, incorrupt! His hand was supple! I dared to kiss it. . . . His

hands gave off water, as though he were alive and perspiring.

The body was intact: skin supple, pink, the face calm and smiling, as though he had simply fallen asleep.

Emmanuel continues:

> The day after I arrived with the father superior in Beirut,[†] people rushed to Annaya. Many miracles and healings occurred through the intercession of Father Charbel, which were reported by the newspapers and mentioned in the records of the monastery.

Father Vaillaume wrote:

> I went personally to Mount Jbeil. It was a marvelous spectacle: dozens of minibuses, hundreds of automobiles were transporting the crowds. It made me think of the crowds that followed the Lord Jesus two thousand years ago. . . . This scene gave the impression of a deep faith! Numerous miracles of conversions took place, even more than the miraculous cures.

---

† At the residence of the Superior General and of Father Mansour Awad, to inform them of the event, given that the tomb had been opened without permission, which could have negative repercussions on the cause of sainthood of Father Charbel.

Conclusion

The Lord Jesus is alive. He cures the wounds of suffering humanity and forgives sins. More than 13,000 miraculous healings, some of them showing physical signs of perpetual cure, as in the cases of Madame Nouhad Al-Chamy and Monsieur Raymond Nader, have been compiled in the records of the monastery in Annaya. The fruits of conversion are innumerable.

HOMILIES

1

Christ is the Truth of Incarnate Love

BEFORE THE BEGINNING there was love. Through it, everything was created from all eternity; without it, nothing would have existed. From the very beginning love existed, which is the foundation of the universe, the law, and the end of all things. Apart from love, nothing will remain, everything will perish.

God is love and truth. God is true love. The universe of God is the world of love, the world of truth; and there is no truth apart from love.

Man is fulfilled only through love; he attains the truth only in God. He belongs to God, because he is the son of love, the son of God, and his true dwelling is in God.

There is a path that leads to the divine world: Christ is this path. He is truth incarnate. He is the manifestation of the truth and of life. Every human being is called to follow this path during his journey in this world toward the next. And since a human being must bring provisions for every journey in this world, the only provision and the only weapon is love. This love can only encompass all human beings gratuitously, without conditions or limits. This is the way in which God loves you. Love one another, therefore, with this same love that is God's love.

Left to himself, man cannot give himself this love. He receives it from God, in Jesus Christ, through the Spirit. In order to do this, it is necessary to pray.

Only through prayer does one acquire the love of God the Father, the source of love, through God the Son, Jesus Christ, incarnate love, through the Spirit of God, the Spirit of love. Pray therefore to have this love so that you might love all men gratuitously, without limits or conditions, as God loves you. You will then be the sons of God. Man is born from the heart of God, and to God's heart he shall return.

2

And You Will Achieve the End For Which You Were Created

WHY DO HUMAN BEINGS have to descend when the path of the Lord ascends? People are loaded down with many burdens that bend their backs so much that their foreheads touch the ground, preventing them from standing up and raising their heads to see the face of God.

They try to liberate themselves from them; everyone gets rid of them only to load themselves down in other ways, and finally they find themselves weighed down with even heavier burdens.

Jesus Christ is the only one capable of liberating all human beings from their burdens, for a slave cannot set another slave free.

A human being is born tied up with cords and bound with chains to which he becomes accustomed throughout his life; many are those who die without being freed from them. People get used to their chains; they cherish them as though they were an integral part of themselves, so that it becomes difficult for them to set themselves free of them.

Their gleaming chains dazzle their eyes so that they no longer see the Lord's face. Their deafening racket prevents them from hearing his voice. They are so proud of the brilliance of their fetters and of their clanking that they cherish them. The chains may well gleam, but they are nonetheless alienating.

Instead of polishing them, break them; instead of making music with them, unfasten them so as to free yourself from them.

The Lord suffers to see the people for whom he was made flesh, died, and rose again in order to give them life and eternal happiness, chained up and seeking their happiness where they will not find it.

Your happiness in this world is not of this world, for if you were of this world you would have remained in it.

Your happiness does not lie in material goods, for they will not procure it for you. Why do men run about seeking gold? A human being is much more valuable than gold! He is the son of God and his value is in himself. Gold does not liberate a human being from his attachments; it only makes them more splendid.

Your happiness does not come from men who cannot offer it to you, because they do not possess it, and because no one can give what does not belong to him. Jesus alone is able to give you true happiness.

Only human beings live between asphalt and concrete. Their minds become blackened like asphalt, and their hearts harden like concrete. Their intellects produce only dark ideas, and their souls become empty of any love. Human beings are like an inert, soulless matter, and some of them resemble stones.

Proud as they are, they stubbornly seek happiness in sin, which causes them nothing but worry, sadness, misery, and emptiness. They have become proud with regard to themselves, towards one another, and towards God.

Do you not realize that the Lord is able to reduce them to dust in an instant? But the love of our God is great. He loves human beings with an unending love because they are his sons and daughters. He wanted them to be the light of the world, in his image.

Every human being is a flame created by our Lord to enlighten the world. Every human being is a lamp made by him to shine and to give light. Someone who obtains a lamp does so in order to light up the darkness. A lamp is made to illuminate darkness.

But these lamps, human beings, are interested only in their appearance: they color their glass panes, cover them with ornaments, whereas God created them plain and transparent so as to protect and propagate the light. They have become thick and hard to the point of hiding the light, and the world remains plunged in darkness.

These lamps that our Lord made to be bearers of light to the world turn themselves into works of art, embellished and tinted but without light. What good is a lamp that does not light up the darkness? You cannot see a lamp in the darkness unless it is lit.

Whatever the beauty of the lamp may be, its light is even more beautiful. The world is going to ruin in the darkness; be its light. Make your glass panes thin and transparent again so as to light up the world and to achieve the purpose for which God created you.

Our Lord has in store a purpose that each creature must fulfill through its life. Contemplate all the creatures on the earth and you will find that each one of them does its work precisely and honestly; not one of them is miserable.

The most miserable creature on earth is surely happier than a sinful human being who, at the moment of judgment, stands shamefaced before the grandeur of God's love: this love that created the universe, that gave life, is the only treasure piled up that will last so as to accompany you into the next world.

All your treasures, your money, and your accomplishments that you think you possess here below, even your bones, will not belong to you any more.

He who appears before the Lord, empty of love, will die of shame. That is his true death and not the moment when he gives up his soul.

If a human being is not transformed by love, he dies, for God is love, a love that is eternal. Let him fill your hearts and let humility govern your minds. Pray and be converted. Pray to Jesus Christ, he will hear your prayer; open your hearts to him, he will enter in and give you peace. Pray from the bottom of your hearts without ceasing.[†]

Do not bother to search for the truth far from Christ; no truth exists outside of him. Christ is the only truth. When you know Christ, you will know the truth and you will be free. Christ wants you to be free. Have no fear, take courage; know that Christ has conquered the world.

† Emending *sans rabâcher*, "without repeating," to *sans relâcher*, "without relaxing or slackening."

3

Your Work
in This World

C HRIST is the way. Stand fast in Christ and persevere along his way; let nothing turn you aside from it.

Allow some time for each of your brethren. Show him the way, direct him toward the light; if he wants to walk alongside you, ask him to go ahead of you; if he wants you to hold his hand, hold both of them; if he tries to lead you astray or to delay you, get away from him, because the way is long. The work is immense.

Sow on earth seeds of prayer, incense, and love. Sow among the rocks, because they may contain a dusting of soil capable of causing what you sow to sprout. If you must crush the rock, strike it without ceasing; if it does not break at the first blow, if will end up being dashed at the hundredth blow. If you grow weary, others will do it instead of you; they will labor and sow. There is a time for sowing and a time for reaping.

Do not be afraid to crumble the rocks, because your arm is yours, but neither the earth nor the axe is yours. Do not moan, do not complain, do not worry.

The ears of grain that are crushed in order to separate the chaff from them complain neither about the weight of the harrow that thrashes the corn, nor about the harshness of the air, because they are preparing to become bread and food. The grapes do not worry when they are crushed and pressed, because they will become wine for joy.

Without crosses you can get neither bread nor wine. Anyone who wants to become bread and wine must carry his cross. Therefore carry your cross and head for the light.

A human being in this world who wants to pass from the dark shore to the shore of eternal light may cross the seas of this world on board many boats:

1. Some are very beautiful, very luxurious, and very comfortable, because they follow their inclinations wherever the wind carries them and their rudders bend with the waves. They do not confront the wind or the waves, because they have no direction and no destination to reach.

These boats draw most people, and they do not go far, because they make no effort to arrive at the right destination. No crossing of the sea of this world is eternal. It always comes to an end, and the passengers on these boats end up at the bottom of the water, not far from the shore from which they set out.

2. The boats of the second sort have thin sails, and

their fragile wood breaks apart on the open sea because of the high waves and the force of the storms. And so their passengers end up somewhere at the bottom of the deep sea.

3. A third sort of boat has hard wood and strong sails and a handsome, attractive form, but the pilot takes his passengers out between deadly shoals. And so the passengers meet their death on one of those shoals from which it is impossible to return.

4. Then too there is the Lord's boat, made of hard wood, with tough sails and a pilot who is full of wisdom, courage, and love. This boat crosses the deep seas, resists the winds and the storms, however violent they may be, and confronts the high waves on the open sea. This voyage is uncomfortable, but it leads you to a safe port.

Be steadfast on the Lord's boat. Do not fear the storms or the high waves. Do not let the luxurious boats attract you to the point of getting on board, because you will miss your destination. Keep in mind the destination that you must reach, rather than the voyage itself. Do not let the depths of the sea charm you. They serve as your means of passage and not as your dwelling place. You cannot be at the same time on board the boat and in the depth of the water, nor on board two boats at the same time.

Stand firm on board the boat of the Lord, and

strengthen your brethren at each port where you land. Invite people to take part in your voyage so as to share with them your arrival at the destination. Speak to them about your pilot and about the shore of light.

But be sure that your words are not the thing that convinces people to come on board the Lord's boat, but rather your confidence, your faith in him, and the joy that is visible on your faces.

Make sure that the voyage on board this boat gives you a face of light so that you live by the light and for it; for man is a universal creature whose limits are those of the light, and not an earthly creature with the limits of dust and water.

A human being is made of dust and light: someone who lives in the dust will return to the dust and die there, whereas someone who lives in the light will return to the light and will live there. Do not let the dust limit you, because the boundaries of your homeland in this world extend toward the places where the sea ends and the sky begins.

Do not allow the dust to enslave you, but be free; freedom lies in liberation from sin. If you are free from sin, nothing can subject you to slavery, whereas if you are slaves of sin, you will be regarded as slaves, even if you hold a royal scepter in your hand.

Stay in a state of grace and stay humble. Be truthful witnesses of Jesus Christ. Return good for evil, but do not take love as an excuse not to confront evil. The plowman does not stop before the stones as an excuse for not working. Have no fear, evil destroys itself.

Become totally involved in the Church and adhere to her teaching. Persevere in prayer without ceasing. Venerate your Mother, the Virgin Mary. Arm yourself with the Rosary, for the name of the Virgin Mary dispels the darkness and crushes evil.

Be monks in the midst of the world, even if you do not wear the habit. Fill the earth with prayer and incense.

Be saints so as to sanctify the earth. The road to sanctity is long, but be assured that if God's thoughts are in your minds and his love is in your hearts, his might will strengthen your arms and you will reach the goal. Be assured that every time you pray, I pray with you to sanctify you; and thus the name of the Lord will be glorified.

4

We Must
Conquer Weakness

EVERY LOCK has its key. Every door has its lock that opens only with the key that belongs to it. Death shut the door and sin bolted it. The cross is the key that frees the lock from sin and the bolt from death; the cross opens the gate of heaven, and there is no other.

The gate of heaven is found where heaven and earth meet, at the summit of Calvary. The gate is well-known, tangible, and visible; everyone has eyes to see it. Some think that it has no lock and that it opens if you push it; but when you draw close to it you understand that it has a lock that opens only with its key. We can know the right key only if it is inserted into the lock. There is only one true key: the cross of Christ.

Do not weary yourself looking for other keys with which to open the gate of heaven, or fabricating others. Many are those who spend their life trying to design their own keys, believing that they would be capable of opening the gate for them; and many too are those who ridicule the cross of Christ. In front of this gate the truth shines forth, and they notice then that all their keys are in vain.

Our whole life is a journey toward this gate, and you will arrive there at the end of your pilgrimage; if you are holding the key in your hand, you will open it and enter. If not, you will stop in front of the gate without being able to go in, because the keys that you have are nothing but your own handiwork. They will disappoint you.

Therefore carry the cross of Christ, and you will have the key to heaven. Carry the cross of Christ with joy, ardor, and courage. Do not weep, do not lament every time you fail. Salvation history is not made up of tears and lamentations, even though the gate of heaven opens only to those who strike their breast and utter cries of lamentation. Salvation history is made up of tears of conversion. Just one tear is enough to open the gate of heaven, the tear of repentance that bathes the cheek of the courageous believer.

Carry the cross of Christ and follow in his footsteps; you will find the Virgin at your side, as she was for Christ. Every time that you feel hurt, say: "By the wounds of Christ." When you suffer, say: "By the sufferings of Jesus." When they persecute you, when they mistreat you or insult you, say: "For the glory of the Lord."

You must conquer your weakness and not make it an

excuse to let yourself go. If you carry the cross of Christ, no suffering can bend you, no weariness can demoralize you; you will walk steadfastly, patiently, silently. Once you have arrived at the gate, you will feel that the joy of your passage far surpasses your suffering and fatigue during the walk. The happiness of your arrival at the destination will infinitely surpass the sorrow of your travels.

The road to your Calvary in this corner of the world is long, and here in the Middle East you carry the cross of Christ on your shoulders. Your enemies are numerous because they are the enemies of the cross; do not take them as enemies; always speak to them with the language of the cross, even if they are hostile toward you because of it.

The months and years to come will be very difficult, bitter and as heavy as the cross. Endure them by praying. May your prayer proceed from your faith, may hope spring from your patience, and may the cross make your love grow.

Violence will reign over all the earth. The planet will be stabbed by the knives of ignorance and hatred. All the nations that surround you will totter under the weight of suffering; fear will beat down on the whole earth like a storm; sadness will overflow from the heart of everyone. Ignorant and hostile men will preside over the destiny of all their peoples, dragging them along the paths of misery and death, because of the blind revenge that they will nickname "justice" and because of the lugubrious ignorance that they will call "faith."

Rancor and ignorance will prevail in all four corners of the world. Resist and stand firm in faith and charity. The face of the earth will change, but you will preserve the face of Christ. Boundaries, communities and regimes will be erased and redrawn, nations will totter beneath the weight of fire and sword; but you will preserve your love without boundaries.

Safeguard your ecclesial community, and may your rule be the Gospel. Be the anchor that holds fast the boats that wander on the turbulent seas; may your hearts be the port of refuge for every human being who is lost, astray, and in need of protection. By your prayers you can bring down the rain of mercy and water the earth with your charity. Pray to soften hardened hearts, to open darkened minds, to comfort those who have experienced catastrophes and horrors.

Finally, have no fear, because the light of Christ will rise and shine, the cross and the Church will illumine each other. Stand fast in your faith in Christ, have no fear, have confidence in the God of the Resurrection and of life. To him be glory eternally.

5

The Center
of the Universe

THE WHOLE UNIVERSE moves around the mystery of the cross. Man believes that the universe revolves around him personally, but the cross is the center of the universe; therefore he who wants to be at the center of the universe must be with the Crucified on the cross. He who does not live the mystery of the cross cannot understand the mystery of the universe.

Every human being has his own form and existence in space and time. He is like a piece of ice that someone tries to keep far from the fire so that it does not melt. What good is this piece of ice if it wants to preserve its form and its being at all costs? If the ice does not melt, it will not be able to soak into the earth to water the land and to quench the thirst of human beings. Do not fear the fire that is capable of making you melt to transform you into life-giving water that irrigates the earth. May your love be like the water that penetrates everywhere, do not let it be like a rigid mass as you yourself have thought of it, a useless form.

Salt that does not dissolve is useless as a seasoning.

Spoiled salt troubles the water and spoils the food; good salt dissolves and disappears in water. It gives neither form nor color to the food, but heightens its flavor. You are the salt of the earth: if you make your life a private property, it will be in vain; whereas if you give it away, its value increases. It will reach its fullness when it is the property of all.

Bread is the same, whether it is on the table of the rich or of the poor. Delicious bread, as it leaves the oven, does not try to find out who will eat it. A good man is a good loaf of bread. Without the cross, the man's story would be empty because it is fleeting. The cross lasts. The cross is what sanctifies you in time.

For God, the beginning of creation and the end of the universe happen together, in the present. If you sanctify the present moment of your life through love, you will realize the mystery of eternity. Through love, man dwells eternally in God.

Sanctify time, sanctify your life through love, sanctify every moment of your life. Do not let the clock distract you, because you cannot stop it; you can only be ready when your hour arrives. If anyone removes God far from his life, his mind, and his heart, time will oppress him and hurl him into death; this does not mean that God does not exist, rather he himself is the one who no longer exists.

As the light shows the eyes what exists, so Christ reveals existence to the mind and the heart. Without light, the human eye does not see what exists. Without Christ, man does not see existence.

God created matter and put it in order; he created the intellect and put spirit into it and gave life. As reason grasps the order and understands matter through logic and analysis, the mind grasps the love of God and the secret of the universe by faith, prayer, and true worship, and gives life.

There are flowers that we pick in the spring as a decoration, while others age and fade to provide new seeds in autumn. There are flowers that disperse their petals to the wind, and their perfume can be smelled far away and almost fills the earth. In every movement God has placed his wisdom; pray, therefore, to understand and to live according to his will, not to change it. The Father's will is always for your good.

Perfume yourselves with the scent of oaks and thyme. Do not wear the colors of this world and do not breathe forth its odors. The actions of God's hand in you are more important that anything this world can clothe you with, which will pass away. Walk at a steadfast pace on the path of sanctity. Let Christ live in you, and then you will live at the heart of the mystery of the universe, in the source of light.

6

Your Journey in This World is an Advance Toward Sanctity

A LL HUMAN BEINGS are endowed with two ears to hear, but very few hear. Among those who hear, there are very few who understand. Then too, among those who hear and understand, there are very few who live in accordance with what they have understood. There are very few who are heading toward the kingdom, and the gate is narrow.

Listen, understand, and witness. Lend an ear to the Savior's voice. Understand the truth and bear witness to it. Live it. Keep silence in order to hear and to understand the Lord's voice. But beware of lending an ear to the echo of your own thoughts; beware of hearing only yourselves. Free yourself from your ideas and let God's word purify them, by cutting away what must be eliminated and by rewriting what must be rewritten.

A human being is a part of a Whole. This part must

listen to this Whole, like a drop of water in the river. The drop cannot be a river, even though it contains everything that makes up the river. The latter is made up of so many drops of water that all follow the same movement. The single drop of water together with the others is a river, but if it withdraws from it, it is only a drop.

Lend an ear to the process of the universe of which you are a part; you will hear that it is on a pilgrimage toward the heart of the Father, like the flowing of the river toward the sea. Do not agree to be outside of this movement. The drop of water that leaves its course cannot be poured into the sea.

Listen and understand the truth, let it penetrate down to your soul.

Break all the layers of the earth's crust, and crumble all the ramparts with which the world has surrounded you, to the point where they have enveloped you and have caused the face of God to shy away.

Be humble and reject all the thoughts that prevent you from hearing his voice, even those that you have devised and cherished.

Listen modestly. May your heart be tender and your mind free. Listening without modesty is like an echo that is lost in the valleys; so what if it is loud? The mountain nonetheless remains a mountain, the valley a valley, and the stone—a stone.

Listen humbly, understand the truth profoundly, and witness modestly. Listen in order to understand and to know.

Live in the light of the truth that you grasp. It is not enough to know the road in order to arrive; you have to follow it. God lights the pages, but it is up to you to read them. God illumines the way for you, but it is up to you to walk in it. Someone who climbs uses his feet, someone who descends does so with his feet; and wherever you arrive, your feet are what brought you there.

Always be listening and on the alert. Do your accounts every day, change your life and renew it. If you listen humbly, you will understand the truth and it will set you free.

Free yourself from the cords that tie you up. Your thoughts, your own beliefs, and your inclinations fetter you like the ropes that immobilize the ship at the dock and secure it, but they do not let it sail.

Let the word of God release you from your bonds by breaking them one after the other, even if it causes you suffering. Do not stagnate in your inclinations and thoughts, even if they offer you rest and security. All security is an illusion without the peace of Christ. Rest far from the heart is a deception. Do not fear to free yourself from the shore and to leave the port; give yourself up to God in order to free yourself from your chains.

His Word is what guides you, and his Spirit is what fills your sails; thus you will arrive at the shore of light. The ship is destined to cross the sea and not to remain in port. It is made to navigate far and wide.

It is necessary to untie all its ropes; if even one of them remains, it will prevent it from leaving the port. Keep only the ropes that raise the mast, the ropes of love and communion that bind you to your brothers, mankind. Your voyage in this world is a path toward holiness, which is a perpetual transformation of the material state toward the state of light.

Pray in order to listen, pray in order to understand, and pray in order to live out your faith, to practice it, and to witness to it. Pray to be transformed into light. Listen while praying, understand the truth in prayer, and live in prayer.

Make sure that your whole life is prayer and service. If you pray without service, you reduce the cross of Christ to a piece of wood by your life. If you serve without praying, you serve each other and yourselves. Pray in your beds, pray as a family, pray in community, in the Church.

Pray in your room in an intimate conversation with the Lord, and you will keep your soul safe, and you will open your intellect to the mystery of God.

Pray as a family, and you will keep your family safe and place it at the heart of the Trinity.

Pray in your community, the Church, and you will keep your Church safe, and you will bring the kingdom of God close.

Your personal prayer in private with the Lord will place you in God's heart. Your prayer together as a family will place you in the bosom of the Trinity. Your community prayer at the heart of the Church will strengthen you in the Body of Christ.

Pray. A man who prays lives out the mystery of existence, and a man who does not pray scarcely exists.

Train yourselves for silence, a silence that listens, a silence that lives, a silence that is quite far from the calm of nothingness.

Practice charity, allow yourself to be transformed by holiness. Listen in order to understand.

Humble yourself in order to understand. Believe and have courage in order to witness.

Love in order to be sanctified.

7

The Lord's House, Founded on Christ

WHEN THE LIGHT of the lantern dims in the middle of the night, it is necessary to fill it with oil. Nowadays the lantern is dimming, the light is going out, and the darkness is mournful. Fill your lanterns before they go out and you are plunged into darkness.

Watch over the lantern that lights your vigils so that it might watch over you and over your houses. Your lanterns dim and your houses grow dark and you limit yourselves to looking straight ahead, neglecting the light that illumines your darkness.

As long as it is night, light up your dark nights with your lanterns. Do not resign yourself to the darkness while waiting for the light of day. When morning rises, another work awaits you and you have to give an account of the night's work.

If the light of your lanterns happens to dim for lack of oil, it is necessary to fill them, instead of going to keep vigil by the light of your brother's while letting your own go out; for you must give an account of your lanterns that light up these vigils and went out. Keep them all lit until it is day.

One fills a lantern with oil and not with wishes, intentions, or even water, thoughtlessly. Be concerned about the light of yours before you think about work and production.

Rethink your priorities to see whether your ladder is not set upside down, the little step at the bottom and the big one at the top.

Look at how the sensible builder erects his house. He puts the big stone at the bottom and the little one on top. At the present hour, many people build their walls in reverse, no longer able to distinguish between the big stone and the little one, the first and the last, the important and the less important.

The wall with the little stone placed at the bottom while the big stone is placed at the top, will collapse, and the house will fall into ruins. Many are the walls that collapse, the rows of stones that disintegrate, because of the ignorance of the laborers and the pride of the builders.

As for you, raise your building wisely. Build on the foundations of Christ, the rock of every house; he holds all the courses of stones together. Place your big stones at the foundation and the little ones above.

If you notice that in one of the walls in your building

there is a big stone above the course and a little one below, it is better to take down the whole wall to rebuild it than to see it collapse entirely on your heads or else on the heads of your brothers or your children.

Be assured that if Christ himself is not the foundation of your whole building, it will collapse. Do not go into ecstasies over a grand house built by human hands; it will collapse, however tall it may be. Time will erase it.

If you discover late that your edifice is not built on Christ, take it down entirely to rebuild it. One course of stones built on Christ is better than a tall tower in danger of being demolished by the winds.

The Lord's house is founded on Christ, and you yourselves are the living stones in it, and the Holy Spirit is the capstone. Christ carries the whole building; the Holy Spirit assembles all the stones of the vaulted ceiling and upholds all the walls. The Spirit is the soul of love, which is the capstone of the arch. If you take away the Spirit, you destroy the capstone; and then the stones will collapse and the whole building will be demolished.

The Holy Spirit is the Spirit of love, the capstone that safeguards the promise. Each stone has its place in the building. Every stone in the course is supported by another one placed beneath it, kept in place by another at its side; it, in turn, supports the others and the ones placed on top of it.

Every stone is designed to stay in its place. If one is missing, it will leave a hole through which the rain, the wind, the dust, and the storms will pass. This hole will allow the external elements to make their way inside. Do not leave a hole between the stones, for the construction will become fragile. Do not leave sand between the stones either, for when the rain and the snow fall and carry off the sand, your building will be ruined. The power of the Spirit is what guarantees that the stone holds together, not the sand.

Stand fast in the Lord's building. Be diligent in building up the kingdom. Be living stones in the temple of the Lord. A stone that is outside this temple is only one stone in a heap of stones. It occupies space but without form, place, or role.

Let yourself be made in the hands of the Lord, the true builder.

Let yourself be carved so as to rid yourself of every superfluous thing and to fill all that is lacking in you. May he himself give you form, volume, and place. Whether you are a big stone or a little one, each one of you has your place for which you were cut out and destined.

Surrender to the Lord, so that he might build. Thus you will take your place in the course of stones, instead of putting yourself in the place that attracts you.

If you choose a place smaller than your volume, you will stick out and be the cause of the dilapidation of the whole wall; if, on the contrary, you choose a place larger than your volume, you will be surrounded by emptiness.

Fill your optimal place. Carry the stones arranged above you, and support those around you. Lean on the one that carries you. Christ carries it all, and the Spirit gathers and guides you.

8

Holiness
is Your Goal

Holiness is your goal. Perfection in love is your final end. Do not stop at the means of holiness so as to idolize them. Do not mistake the means for the end, nor the end for the means. Do not make the means your goal and your final end; do not make use of holiness as a means to achieve other ends.

Prayer sanctifies you; do not sanctify it. Fasting strengthens you; do not make it a god. Mortifications purify you; do not adore them. Your chanting is designed to praise God, but do not glorify it.

Do not exchange Christ for your talk about him, for in that way you will adore what you say. Do not identify the expressions with the truth, because these utterances will pass for the truth. For you, the word will never be more important than the idea that it expresses, nor the thought more important than the truth that it contains.

The safe can never be more important than the treasure that it contains, nor the glass more important than the wine that it contains, nor the bakery more important than the bread, nor the tabernacle more important than the Blessed Sacrament.

Christianity is neither the religion of the temple nor the religion of the book. Christianity is the person of Jesus Christ himself. The mirror that reflects the light is not the light. It is necessary to distinguish between the light and the mirrors that reflect it. Do not concentrate on the mirror. Fix your hearts on the light.

Do not shirk your own responsibilities in order to take refuge in God. Do not seek refuge in God in order to flee from yourself. God wants you to offer yourself to him as you are in order to elevate you and sanctify you. Do not let the world push you toward God. Allow God to attract you to him.

Do not blacken with your writings the white pages written by your holy Fathers. The truth is always the same. In order to speak about God, it is necessary for him to be in your heart; for you cannot talk about God while you are far from him.

The word is a body and not a voice fluttering in the sky. Before saying your word, cut it with your reason, sculpt it in your souls, reread it in your heart and make it issue from your mouth as though you were putting the stone at its correct place in the course.

Give up any word that is not constructive. Speak only when your speech proves to be more profound and more eloquent than your silence. Do not allow your talk about the deep sea to prevent you from sailing on it.

Aim for the essence. Distinguish in your life between what is essential and what is superficial, between fundamentals and secondary matters, between the kernel and the shell.

In your life, do not put water into a basket, nor grapes into a jug, nor figs into a jar. Since you are capable of making prudent use of the things of the earth, learn also how to treat the things of heaven, with the Lord's wisdom, for your salvation and for God's glory.

Every land has its soil, its climate, and the tools with which to work it in order to sow it and to plant the kind of trees that grow there and bear fruit. You cannot break the rocks with a pitchfork, nor turn over the soil with a sledgehammer, nor cut wood with a shovel. The cedars and the oaks do not grow in the sand of the seashore, nor banana and orange groves among the rocks on the mountain. Do your work with the available tools, and flourish and bear your fruit where God planted you. If you are not rooted, you cannot raise yourself up.

Adapt your minds to reality and not reality to your minds. Reality existed before you and it will remain after you. Only the Spirit governs you and harmonizes you with God.

Thanks to the light of the eternal Spirit who is in you, you can realize the depth of the mystery of existence. Do not seek to understand the truth through your senses, for you will run up against the limits of these senses.

Know that they help you to love, but do not love them. If you love your sight, you will adore the creatures that you see, forgetting the Creator who is beyond your eyes.

If you love your hearing, you will be in love with the melodies and sounds of this world, forgetting to listen to God's voice in the silence that is inaudible to your ears.

If you love your sense of smell, you will be drawn by the perfumes of the world, forgetting the flowers of the fields that the Lord, in his goodness, created for you.

If you love your sense of taste, you will be prisoners of eating and drinking, forgetting the food that nourishes the soul.

If you love your sense of touch, you will be prisoners of the exterior, turning away from the interior. Go beyond your senses and you will not drown in them. Go beyond them to reach the truth like the rays of light that penetrate the crystal.

If you toughen your senses, they will thicken and you will reflect the world's images as mirrors send back the light. Do not drown in your senses; do not be fooled by the joy that they procure for you.

True joy is not in the senses: it consists of going beyond them so as to infiltrate into the heart of the light, to the place where you plunge into the heart of God, where you contemplate his light and are fused with his love.

Every time that you want to look at the exterior, close your eyes and look to the interior; that is when you will see the exterior more clearly.

Every time that want to hear, close your ears and listen to the interior voice; then you will hear better.

Master your senses so as to glorify God, and do not let them lead you to glorify his creatures.

Love even unto the gift of yourself. Blood is the only ink with which love is written; the rest is just ink on paper. In Christ, every human being is a word in God's mouth until all humanity becomes a hymn of love. Glory to God.

9

Your Destiny
is the First Day
in the Next World

CONSIDER HOW the birds of the air painstakingly build their nests; they very bravely lay their eggs in them and watch tenderly over their little ones until they have their plumage and can fly. They preserve the trees of the Lord.

As for you, you build your nests, you lay your eggs, and your hatchlings see the light of day in trees whose roots are rotted with the blight that eats away at them, while worms gnaw at their trunks and their leaves. If the tree falls, your nests will be ruined, your hatchlings will be scattered, and you will have only naked branches on which to rest your wings.

You weary yourselves, you toil to build warm, sturdy nests in which your hatchlings can grow up, fly away, and make their own nests in turn.

Care for the tree with the same care that you devote to the nest. Just as you take charge of your nests, take charge of your trees also. Care for the roots, the trunk, the branches, and the leaves. All you need are a few tools with a handful of earth in order to set up your nests. Besides, the branches of the tree protect you and the leaves shade you.

Do not worry about building up your nests with high edges so as to find security in them; work while entrusting yourselves to the Lord who will take care of you.

Do not work anxiously to secure your future and that of your children. Remember that you will have secured your children's future when you assure them of Heaven.

You must give life to your children. Now, there is no life except in Christ. Therefore offer them Christ. But if he is not in you, it will be difficult for you to give him to them.

If your do not sanctify yourselves, how do you think you will sanctify your children? If you do not lead them to Christ, everything that you have offered them will be sterile and perishable. They themselves will perish with all those perishable possessions. Neither the fortresses nor the guarantees of this world will be able to obtain security and a future for your children. Your sanctity and your prayers are what they need for their security in this world and for their future in the next.

You run after your success and that of your children, for their future, but success in life consists of standing without shame before God. Sink down to the roots and make sure of this, with asceticism. The work of taking root is hidden, it will not appear, and it requires effort and asceticism. Men do not see your efforts and your troubles; God who is in heaven sees and blesses.

Look after the soil, watch the branches, treat the leaves, guard the tree so that God will preserve your work. Guard the tree and God will guard your actions. Take care of the tree that shelters you, gives you its shade, and protects you, from its roots to the end of its branches, even if it means that your nests will not be as high.

The same time passes for the good as for the wicked. If the former do not fill it with good deeds, the latter will sow evil in it until they make it useless.

Every moment of your life is considered a basket that is entrusted to you to fill it with your harvest and with your fruits. This instant is brief; it disappears into the past, forever irreversible. If you stop to look behind you and find that your baskets are empty, only the tears of your conversion are capable of filling them, through the mercy and grace of God. This grace is enough for you at every second, so that you might fill it with God and it might become a drop of eternity.

Do not let the world steal from you the baskets of

your life and leave them empty. That is how you accumulate the heaps of straw that time is capable of burning, only to leave nothing.

Do not enter into a dialogue with the devil. Put an end to the conversation before the first word. Always dialogue with God.

Repair your roofs well after each winter in order to avoid leaks. For if you fail to do it, the downpours and the snow will beat on them, the water will trickle from your terraces and penetrate into the beams; thus your roofs will collapse on your heads and those of your children.

However attractive the temptation may be, it cannot justify sin. May your life be filled with the love of God. Sanctify your time so that your harvest may be abundant and your provisions will not run out. Only the Lord of the harvest and of the produce can fill your baskets. Offer them to him and your harvest will increase.

10

Rest is a Danger

THE KINGDOM OF GOD is like the construction site of a temple whose building stones come from rocks taken from the quarries of this world. Human beings are the workers on the site at God's decree, and the builders build according to his will. They hew the stones from the rocks taken from the quarries and place them stone upon stone, one after the other. And God breathes life into them so that human beings become living stones of this temple.

Many men build their own temple with the stones hewn from the rocks and claim to be their owners. They build them stone by stone, one after the other, without being able to give them life, however, because God alone is capable of providing it. Those people perish, leaving behind them the stones, rocks, and quarries, as well as their little temples built of dead stones. Subject to deterioration, they are annihilated over time. They too are perishable along with their temples.

Only the temple of the Lord is eternal because it is alive. Build up this eternal temple and be living stones in it, instead of raising your little fleeting temples with dead stones that time will ruin. Work diligently, joyfully, cooperatively, and lovingly; do so with patience, humility, and obedience to the Lord of the temple. Since you work by his decree, build according to his will.

Build well without growing weary. Do not seek rest, because that is the source of a great danger for you. If you see an idle worker, do not criticize him, do not condemn him, and do not curse him. On the contrary, with your pick or your sickle in hand, continue your work; thus you will oblige him to work, because the building belongs to both of you. The harvest is yours and his, and the whole thing belongs to the Lord of the temple and to the God of the harvest.

Respect your fellow man as you respect yourself. There is always in you something of what you see in your brother, because the other is you with a few differences. Instead of speaking against your brother, go and speak with him; if not, then kindly keep quiet.

Never condemn, and do not judge by what your eyes see. You cannot pass judgment on the water that you see in a glass, because with your eyes you cannot tell whether it is fresh or salty, drinkable or insipid.

To outward appearances, jars of wine are all alike, even if the wine inside is not the same. Look at the outside with your eyes, but at the inside with your hearts. The heart does not condemn.

Do not claim to have absolute knowledge and thus build temples by the measure of the things that you know; they will fall down on your heads and kill you. Knowledge needs love in order to become understanding.

However great your knowledge may be, you cannot understand as long as you do not love. Love is much nobler than intellect. The logic of love is much more sublime than that of the intellect.

Knowledge without love lacks soul; it destroys a human being. The earth is a sanctified globe on which the God of the universe has set his foot. He has illuminated it with the light of the Spirit, and his divine Heart watches over it.

With their loveless knowledge, human beings have made the earth sick. Their food poisons them, their drink makes them thirsty. They mistake their illnesses for medications; the air that they breathe stifles them, their food tires them, their peace causes them anxiety, their joy saddens them, their happiness torments them, their truth is an illusion and their illusion is truth, their light darkness.

Human beings have more knowledge than wisdom. Their theories have become in their minds like the fog on the mountains and in the valleys; they prevent them from seeing things as they are. Their theories rob them of sight.

Their buildings rise, their morality sinks. Their worldly goods increase, their values diminish. Their speeches multiply, their prayers grow scarce. Their interests deepen, their relationships wear thin; their façades expand, their interiors become impoverished. Their roads are broadened, their vision becomes shortsighted.

They have many paths, but they do not lead them to each other's houses. They have multiple means of communication, but they do not help them to communicate with each other. Their beds are spacious and comfortable, but their families are small, broken up, and exhausted. They know how to go faster without being able to wait. They are always running to make a living, forgetting to lead their lives.

They hurry toward the outside and neglect what is inside. They are prisoners who take pride in the comfort of their prisons, lost travelers who boast of the distances that they have covered, dead men who flatter themselves with the luxuriousness of their tombs. They die of hunger while sitting next to the kneading trough, poor men, yet sitting on the treasures that they themselves have buried.

Why do you take a place beneath the table to eat the

crumbs that fall from it when the meal is being served for you? Human beings sow thorns which, while still tender and new, caress their feet; but once they have hardened they will tear the feet of future generations.

You cut the wood, you pile the logs, you light the fire, you feed it so as to throw yourselves into it, and you wonder why you are burned by it! Humanity has gone astray, man is sick, and the world is catching fire.

God is love; he is the goal and guide of this lost humanity. Christ is the remedy of the sick man. The water of baptism in the Spirit is what extinguishes the fire raging in the world.

Base all of your knowledge on Christ; all knowledge built apart from the foundation of Christ will condemn you. All knowledge without soul is considered ignorance.

An edifice based on man may well rise, but it ends up crushing him. Man lives in sadness and anxiety; he is satisfied and fulfilled only when he is unified in the heart of God.

Meet one another, look at one another, listen to one another, greet one another, console one another with sturdy, charitable words, go out from yourselves to visit one another, embrace one another in the love of Christ, work in the Lord's field without growing weary or bored.

May the sound of your picks fill the valleys and drown out the noise of the world, and may the sound of your scythes' call remind people of the harvest.

May your prayers split the deaf rocks and cause the mute springs to gush forth. The rocks hear prayer, the springs speak about it, and together they all pray and glorify God.

11

Travel the Path With the Joy of the Resurrection

Y OU WALK ALONG the path of your life, carrying the weight of burdens and many cares, loaded with all sorts of jars; some of them useful, others useless, while scattering your treasures in them.

You mix up your treasures with your junk, and you no longer know where, in what jar they are. The jars are so cumbersome that some of them fall and are broken, some treasures are lost. Some people fritter away their fortune along the path of their life and arrive loaded down only with clay.

Every jar you carry that does not contain your treasure is a useless burden full of distractions, which slows your march and tires you.

Get rid of the jars that the world obliges you to carry, even if you have carried them during a long, tiring journey and perhaps have become accustomed to them.

Know where your treasure is and put your whole heart there; store it all in just one jar and carry it carefully. Thus you will preserve it, and you will arrive rich with this treasure.

Carry just one jar, the jar of Christ, who enriches you with love and carries it with you. Even when it is full, it will always be able to hold more; although heavy, it will be easy to carry.

The other jars are all made of clay; even when empty they will be difficult to carry and will bend your back. Choose for yourselves your paths in this world, and do not let the path choose you. Do not carry the jars that the world imposes on you to distract and exhaust you.

The more your jars multiply, the more remote you will be from your neighbor. Each one of them demands a distance. The more numerous they become, the greater the distances around you, and you will be obliged to distance yourselves from one another so that your jars do not collide and run the risk of breaking. Therefore the jar becomes more important than your brethren. In your anxiety to protect your jars, you will have lost your brethren and your neighbors.

Know that your treasures are very precious, but that you carry them in an earthen vessel, and all your brethren own a precious treasure, and they too carry it in an earthen vessel.

You make your jars with your own hands and shut

yourselves up in them, telling yourselves: "The world is made of clay." Someone who puts himself inside the jar sees all of life as though it were made of clay. Come out of it and see the world as it is, and not as you have imagined it from inside. Let everyone fill his jar with the treasure of Christ, who is the only true treasure.

Be full grains of wheat on the Lord's threshing floor so that you may have weight and fall when the fork winnows you and you may be gathered up so as to be stored in the barns of life. Do not be light, empty grains like the straw that the wind carries off far from the threshing floor and scatters. Only Christ can fill you and give you weight.

Be filled with Christ so that you can remain on the threshing floor and be gathered up. As long as you remain on the threshing floor, the shovel will keep winnowing you to remove the straw from you. Every grain of wheat remains alone, even if it is gathered with the others in the measure and in the sack.

The mill, the water, and the fire make the flour into one lump of dough and one loaf. It is a long process from the field to the bread. Pray for the sickle that cuts you down, for the flail that threshes you, for the threshing floor that gathers you, for the fork that winnows you, for the mill that grinds you, for the water that kneads you, and for the fire that bakes you.

The path of sanctity extends from the field to the bread, from the dust to the light, from the crib to the cross.

Travel it with the joy of the resurrection.

12

Holiness is Not Luck; Holiness is a Choice

MEN DEMAND MIRACLES in order to believe, signs in order to see, messages in order to hear and understand, a path in order to walk and to reach salvation and happiness.

The miracle is the Blessed Sacrament, the sign is the cross, the message is the Gospel, salvation is in the Church.

The most important, the noblest, and the holiest sign is the cross, which is the sign of God's love for you. Make it also the sign of your love for him. It is a sign of love and not of trouble; its light will shine upon the whole world.

The salvation of humanity is accomplished by the Church, which for two thousand years has been carrying out the plan of which Christ is the beginning, and it will not be finished before the end of the world. All the waves of evil will break against the rock of the Church. Commit yourself fully to it, and do not pick and choose among its teachings.

The most important and greatest message is the Gospel, which conveys Christ's teaching; not a single letter of it will fall before the world perishes. Anyone who does not know the Gospel is an ignorant person who lives in darkness, even if he possesses all the knowledge in the world. Anyone who does not conform himself to the Gospel does not live. Do not falsify it to justify yourself. The reality of the Gospel is always the same.

The most important miracle is the Blessed Sacrament, the Body of Christ, the Paschal Lamb who takes away the sins of the world, the living God who has risen from the dead.

It is vain to look for signs more important than the sign of the cross. Do not demand messages that you suppose are more important than that of the Gospel. Do not seek your salvation far from Christ's Church. Do not become distracted by running after dazzling miracles greater than that of the Blessed Sacrament. Forsake the deceptive magic that only sends you back into emptiness. Avoid any sign that does not point you to the sign of the cross. Ignore any message that does not come from the Gospel. Reject any miracle that does not bring you before the Blessed Sacrament.

In the Church you discern all these signs. Through the cross, the Gospel, the Blessed Sacrament, and in the Church, you sanctify yourselves. God predestined you to holiness and not to death. Holiness is not luck; holiness is a choice.

Do not expect it to be offered to you from outside; it is necessary to live it and to realize it inside. The kingdom of heaven is within you. Holiness is a grace and a decision: the grace is given to you by God, and it is up to you to make your decision. You are potentially saints; strive to be saints in reality.

13

Love is a
Radiant Light

Love is not an attachment, because it is freedom, whereas an attachment enslaves. God is freedom.

Love must not be taken solely as a human affection; it is a divine force of creation, a force of heavenly resurrection.

Love is not an instinct that springs from the material senses; it is a force of life gushing from the Spirit.

Love is not a dead habit that binds and attaches you; it is a force of perpetual renewal that revives and frees you.

Love is not a feeling aimed in a particular direction; it is a light radiating in all directions.

God is neither a feeling nor an affection nor a habit nor an attachment nor an idea. He is Reality and Life, and a Creator who gives life.

Love is gratuitous, and to be given it demands nothing in return; it is always oriented toward the other. The love that comes from a human being returns to him. When the love springs from the human being himself, he loves himself, whatever the strength of that love may be. However, if a human being draws his love from God, he is naturally oriented towards others. If the love is from you, it returns to you. The human being whose love emanates from himself loves himself through others, while thinking that he loves others.

Never confuse love and desire, love and affection, love and habit, love and attachment.

14

Acknowledge Your Sins So As to Kill the Evil That is in You

WHEN JESUS CHRIST was raised up, the devil fell down. Anyone who clings to the devil falls with him. He who stands on his path runs the risk of falling. Never cling to the devil, and never set out on his path.

His only concern is to falsify the image of God in your minds and to ruin you. He wants you to think of God in a false way and to make the mistake of looking at yourselves.

He falsifies, distorts, and deceives. He tries to puff you up when you should humble yourselves and humiliate you when you should grow. He tries to stop you when you should walk and make you walk when you should stop, to make you talk when you should keep silence and hush you when you should speak, to convince you to go faster when you should slow down and slow down when you should run.

In any case, he seeks to fool you. The devil is the

biggest liar, the greatest of all frauds, crooks, and hyp-ocrites; as the Lord described him: "He is a liar and the father of lies."

The devil never shows his true face. He knows what man likes and what attracts him; he presents to him what he likes and what attracts him. He speaks to you about what you would like to hear. He shows you the things that you would like to see. He offers you the things that you would like to touch. He gives you to eat the things that you would like to taste.

When counterfeiters fake gold, they do it with the same brilliant color. It is the same with the devil who, when he wants to fake the image of the God of love, resorts to things that human beings call love in order to cause confusion, to muddle the reality of the God of love in man's mind. He plays on our instinct and affec-tions, on our ties and attachments, and on the slavery of our habits.

The devil's only interest is to hinder those who are walking toward the Lord. As you travel, he strives to:

> 1. Make you stray from the path, by inventing for you a goal that attracts you and obliges you to go in his direction; thus you will wander and get lost.

> 2. Make you fall by setting a trap for you to fall into.

3. Make you go back: he wearies you and drives you to despair and to give up; he wants to prevent you from arriving.

Everything that gathers and unifies for the good is the work of God. On the contrary, everything that divides and separates comes from the devil. He dominates man by means of the things in life. The more you get rid of them, the better you are protected against him. Conversely, the more you become attached to them, the more subject you are to the power of evil.

The devil is the lord of this world; the more you plunge into it, the more you come under his dominion; you may as well get rid of it so as to be free. Do not forget that you are not of this world, do not drown in it. Make your journey through it, stand up, and you will lift the world toward the Lord by the power of Christ hanging on the cross.

At first the devil makes a man laugh so as to make him weep afterward. He leads him to hell by always making him laugh—hence the weeping and the gnashing of teeth. The man who laughs now with the devil will surely end by weeping.

Does God make you weep at first? He will make you rejoice at the end. God makes you weep in order to correct you; the devil's role is to make you laugh so as to separate you from God. When God makes you laugh, the devil interferes to make you weep; do not be fooled.

The devil hates the image of God and the human being who receives it. He wants to deform this image in man. To do that, the only method is to stop the work of the Spirit of God in man; then the only image that remains is that of the animal.

The first indispensable weapon against the devil is sincerity. Every sincere word is an arrow shot into the heart of evil. Every sincere confession is a lance that pierces its heart.

The second indispensable weapon is humility; sincerity and humility mean confession. Make your confession in order to kill the evil in you.

The devil seeks to turn you away from God. Be careful! He tries to rob you of God through the very things of God. He distracts you from the Name of the One to whom you pray. He distracts you from praising the Lord with the melody or hymn with which you praise him; he distracts you from God with the prayer that you address to Him.

Remember well that you cannot confront the devil unless you get down on your knees before God. The devil does not use windows and skylights that you close securely; he comes through the door that you leave open to welcome people…

15

Movement and Life

THERE IS A big difference between movement and life. Man can be in movement without, however, really living. He can also possess life and lack movement. Man is made of movement and life. The whole universe with its galaxies, stars, and numerous creatures is in movement, but it is not necessarily true that it possesses life or that this movement is always a life. Life is only in God the Creator. God is life.

Every movement in the universe is subject to death, but life is eternal. However great it may be, every movement comes to an end; life has no end. Life is eternal because God is life. Movement perishes, but life is imperishable. Man has within himself movement and life.

Movement is determined by space and time, whereas life is limited neither by time nor by space. Man's movement is subject to death and comes to an end even if it lasts a long time, but life is eternal.

Christ came to give us life and to sanctify the movement in us. He gives us eternal life, because he is the Son of God, and life is from him.

Without Christ, our movement is condemned to inevitable death; with him, we have eternal life. We cannot be somewhere between the two, it is necessary to choose: death or life.

Sanctify the movement that is in you by means of the life that is from Jesus Christ. Do not seek to perpetuate yourself in this world by prolonging your movement to infinity. For even time will come to an end.

Immortality resides in eternal life in Jesus Christ. There are no immortal movements in time because it is not eternal.

16

Every Family
is a Holy Family

THE HUMAN FAMILY on earth is an image of the
divine family in heaven. This is what transmits
God's plan from one generation to another. This is
what spreads God's love and his word down through
the generations.

The collapse of the family means the ruin of the
Lord's plan for humanity, that is to say, a breakdown
that removes salvation and sanctity from human beings.

Every family is a Holy Family because it is in the
image of the Triune God. The deformation of the family means the deformation of God's image. The family
carries the torch and the Book from generation to generation so that the world might continue to be illuminated by the light of the Lord.

The family is the cord that ties human beings to one
another through history, so that humanity might grow
and multiply. If this cord is cut and humanity is sepa-
rated from its history, the generations will be lost
without history or identity.

The family gives humanity its human identity and imprints the image of God on it. It safeguards human memory. Men without a family are mankind without a memory. Man deprived of memory goes around in circles. Humanity without memory stagnates in history and dies.

The family is the basis in the Lord's plan, and all the forces of evil aim to demolish it, because they know that in destroying it they will shake the foundations of God's plan.

The war of the Evil One against the Lord is a war waged against the family. This latter war is the essence of his war against the Lord, because the family is the image of God. Since the beginning of the creation of this universe, the wicked one has persistently tried to destroy the family, which is the foundation of God's plan.

The family is the place where a human being enters into communication with God and with his brethren. Without the family, this relationship would be destroyed and nothing could compensate for it, and if a man tries to repair the relationship by human means, it will become fragile and misguided, and along with that, all humanity will be subject to an evil that will tilt it toward inevitable death.

Uphold your families and guard them against the grudges of the Evil One by the presence of God. Protect them and preserve them by prayer and dialogue, by understanding and forgiveness, by sincerity and fidelity, and most importantly by listening.

Listen to one another with your ears, with your heart, with your mouth, and with the palms of your hands. Keep your hands far from the hustle and bustle of the world, because it will sweep away and destroy everything like a raging storm and the violence of waves when they come back into a house. Safeguard the warmth of the family, because all the warmth of the world will not make up for it.

17

Wisdom and Parables

THE SHEPHERD'S STAFF serves to guide the flock and to protect it against the wolves and the beasts of the forest. The good shepherd, even though he carries a crozier, should consider it a staff; an oaken crook becomes a crozier in the hand of a good shepherd, and a jewel-encrusted crozier remains a crook in his hand.

The thimble and the cauldron, when full, resemble each other. Whether you are a cauldron or a thimble, the essential thing is that you be full. Always seek fullness, whichever you may be.

When the world crumbles, truth is still standing. The world never gives you anything except promises; God alone delivers.

You cannot lift people up higher than yourself. You can climb so as to draw them toward you; the more you climb, the more you draw your brethren toward you. Christ lifted you up when He was lifted up; you will lift up your brethren if you lift yourself up by Christ's power. If you climb toward Him, you will draw with you all who are alongside you.

Do you sell your souls in the markets of this world? They are very precious; whatever price the world sets for you, it is laughable compared with their true value. Do not sell them, because the world cannot pay you the price for them, which is the blood of Christ, entirely poured out on the cross.

The kingdom of God is not an end but a journey that you make within you by the power of the Spirit—step by step, over the course of the days, and in the little details that fill the moments of your life, second by second.

Meditation consists of contemplating things as they are, and not as you think them to be in your mind, or as you want them to be.

You like the mental image that you have made for yourself about a person and not the person himself; you detest the idea that you formed about him and not the person himself. Beware, do not judge, do not form ideas about anyone at all. Prejudices are the tinted lenses through which you see others with a color that is not theirs.

Put the wisdom of nature into your mind, its beauty into your heart, and its perpetual power to renew into your spirit.

When you commit a sin, acknowledge it; admit your fault, confess it, and correct yourself as well as you can. An error once admitted makes you great and does not belittle you. Correct what you can; confess the rest to God, who will set right what is incorrigible and make amends for what is irretrievable.

Do not justify your sin by your good intentions, for they will not bring you to heaven. Your works must be as good as your intentions; what matters are the fruits of your acts and the consequences of your words, and not your good intentions. A good intention is the argument of the ignorant person, and ignorance is like sleep from which it is necessary to awaken in order to realize that one was sleeping. Wake up those who have fallen asleep and, after they have awakened, they will understand that they were sleeping. Do not speak with a sleeper, for he will not hear you; wake him up first, then speak with him.

The more holiness grows in a human being, the less he grasps it, and when he becomes aware of his holiness, it vanishes.

Turn the word over in your head, as the thrower swings the stone around with the sling and does not let it loose until he is sure that he has aimed it at the target. The word in your mouth is like the stone in the sling: if you launch it, you will not be able to bring it back again; if your word is not aimed at the target, it will do harm; if the word is inadequate, it will hurt. Avoid the use of words with several meanings; use the word that allows only one interpretation. Be a good example instead of giving good advice.

Every time you see a fault, correct it silently instead of rebuking it verbally.

Whether the stone is in the open air, exposed to the sun, or in the river hidden in the water, or immersed in perfume, or surrounded with incense, or coated thickly with paint, it remains a stone. A rock produces only rubble, stones and sand; and however you may polish it, at best you get nothing but dust from it.

It is always necessary to discern carefully between your desires and your needs. A human being wants many things that he does not need, and he lacks many things that he does not desire. Your worth is measured by what you are and not by the abundance of your possessions. What you think you possess in this world is what possesses you in reality; what you think is under your dominion in the world is what dominates you in reality. In all the things that you master, you are the devil's associate; you exist in this world to give and to serve, not to possess, dominate, and command.

There is a big difference between signing up and being committed. Living a life of commitment in the Church is not the same as registering with the parish community.

The direction that you start out in is more important than the speed you set; what good is your velocity and acceleration if you have chosen the wrong direction?

Begin nothing on earth unless it has its end in heaven; do not walk on a path that does not lead to heaven.

Your five senses are incomplete; your common sense completes them.

You cannot be a saint without becoming a human being first.

The things that go on within you are more important than those that take place in your life.

Always distinguish between an occasion and a temptation. Seizing an occasion is different from surrendering to a temptation; for seeking to profit from an occasion is an initiative for the good, whereas giving in to temptation is a tumble toward evil.

Sin is like poison, sinning is taking poison; for certainly you are the one who will be poisoned. And then it makes little difference how you ingested it or who gave it to you; when you poison yourself and die, it will be useless to blame others.

The ignorant man hangs on to dust until he becomes dust; the wise, sensible man heads for heaven until he reaches it. You belong to the place that you are fond of.

All that enters into you, and all that you receive, does not belong to you; on the contrary, what emanates from you and what you give is yours. Your esteem does not lie in what you receive, but in what emanates from you. What people give you does not become who you are; you will be yourself in what you give. You possess nothing of what you bring into yourself; transform it all into sanctity emanating from you, by the power of the Spirit, and it will be capable of giving you everything as your possession.

On the Lord's path, if you go back one step, the devil makes you retreat ten; if you go forward one step, the Lord will help you to take a hundred.

The man who spends his life ringing the church bell is not the one who will necessarily go to heaven and save his soul. The best thing is for him to hear the bell of his conscience when it tolls sin; many are those who ring the church bell so as not to hear the bell of their conscience.

Do not eat to the point of satiety, eat to silence your hunger; for a human being knows when he is no longer hungry but does not know when he can satisfy himself. There are no limits to human satisfaction.

The sweetness of chastity is more delightful than sexual pleasure.

What inebriates a human being is not wine; it is always the human being who makes himself drunk.

Printed in Great Britain
by Amazon